UNDERSERVED PRIVILEGE

Mandy Adebayo, Ph.D.

Underserved Privilege

Copyright © 2024 by Mandy Adebayo, Ph.D.

Notice of Copyright

Author:

Mandy Adebayo, PhD.
mandyadebayo68@gmail.com
+2348033112590 | +2348099587425

Publisher:

BLUEINK AFRICA (Print copy)
info@bluinkafrica.com | blueinkafrica@gmail.com
+234(0) 808 888 4786 | +234(0) 806 222 9837
Printed in The Federal Republic Nigeria
First Printing Edition, 2024
Image on the cover was from Freepik.

Because of our faith, Christ has brought us into this place of undeserved privilege where we now stand, and we confidently and joyfully look forward to sharing God's glory.

Romans 5 verse 2 (NLT Bible)

CONTENTS

DEDICATION

For my beloved husband, who has been my constant source of strength and inspiration. Your love makes everything possible.

ACKNOWLEDEMENT

A special thank you to my family, for the countless hours of support and encouragement. You have been my rock through it all. I want to also say thank you to my readers— you are the reason this book exists, and I am eternally grateful for your support.

INTRODUCTION

Salvation—the great promise that captivates our hearts. In the depths of Scripture, we discover the unfolding of God's redemptive plan for humanity. We read with wonder of Christ's sacrifice that tore the veil between us and paved the way for new life. The old passed away; the new has come.

The words of Acts 4:12 echo through the corridors of time: "There is salvation in no one else, for there is no other name under heaven given to people by which we must be saved." Jesus alone holds the keys to redemption. He alone can rescue us from the entanglements of sin and darkness.

As II Corinthians 5 unpacks, we glimpse the magnitude of God's love: "God made Him who knew no sin to become sin on our behalf so that in Him we might become the righteousness of God." Though perfect in every way, Jesus willingly bore our sins upon Himself, exchanging them for His righteousness. By grace we are saved, transformed, born again into new creations. The penalty of sin dissolved; our status changed forever.

This new birth in Christ ushers us into the family of God. When we confess Jesus as Lord and believe God raised Him from dead, we receive the gift of salvation. By faith, we are brought into the undeserved privilege of daughtership and sonship. As John 4 proclaims, "As He is, so are we in this world." The old nature fades as Christ's eternal life sparks within us. Sin's grip is broken; purity breathes in our lungs.

Indeed, God has given us eternal life through His Son alone. As 1 John 5 testifies, "Whoever has the Son has this life; whoever does not have the Son of God does not have life." Life pulses through our veins by grace alone through faith alone in Christ alone. Simon Peter thus cried, "Lord, to whom would we go? You have the words that give eternal life."

In Christ, we discover the power and wisdom of God, as 1 Corinthians 1 illuminates. Union with Jesus aligns every aspect of our lives with truth. Righteousness, holiness, and divine purpose begin to blossom as we walk hand-in-hand with our Savior. Truly, we can live assured of the eternal life He grants to all who believe.

This, dear one, is the gift set before you—life everlasting by faith in the Son of God. Receive the riches Christ longs to lavish upon you. Taste the goodness of knowing Him deeply, living in union with the God who is Love. As John 5 reminds, the Son has come that we might know the One True God.

In Jesus, eternal life awaits. Will you believe?

CHAPTER ONE

PROPHECY OF JESUS' BIRTH

In the sacred scriptures, we find profound prophecies that speak of the extraordinary birth of Jesus, the long-awaited Messiah. These verses, filled with divine wisdom and foresight, offer us a glimpse into the remarkable plan of God for the redemption of humanity.

Let us first delve into the words of the prophet Micah, who declares, "But you, Bethlehem Ephratah, though you be little among the thousands of Judah, yet out of you shall he come forth unto me that is to be ruler in Israel, whose goings forth have been from of old, from everlasting." It is awe-inspiring to think that from this seemingly insignificant town would emerge the ruler of Israel, whose origins trace back to eternity itself. God, in His infinite wisdom, chose Bethlehem as the birthplace of the long-awaited Messiah, demonstrating His ability to work through the humblest of circumstances.

Turning our attention to the words of Isaiah, we encounter a prophecy that brings hope and reassurance to the people of Israel. The prophet speaks to the house of Daniel, reminding them that God is not wearied by the burdens of mankind. He declares, "Therefore, the Lord himself shall give you a sign: Behold, a virgin shall conceive, and bear a son, and shall call his name Immanuel." These words echo throughout the ages, assuring us that a miraculous birth would take place—a child conceived by a virgin, who would be called Immanuel, meaning "God with us." This extraordinary sign would signify the coming of the Messiah, who would bridge the gap between God and humanity, bringing divine presence and salvation.

Further along in Isaiah, we encounter a prophecy that unveils the nature and authority of the promised child. The prophet declares, "For unto us a child is born, unto us a son is given: and the government shall be upon his shoulder: and his name shall be called Wonderful, Counsellor, The Mighty God, The Everlasting Father, The Prince of Peace." These majestic titles bestowed upon the Messiah reveal His divine attributes and the profound impact He would have on the world. He would be a source of wonder, a wise counsellor, the mighty God Himself, an eternal father, and the bringer of peace—a true embodiment of God's love and grace.

The Gospel of Matthew provides us with another vital piece of the puzzle. It recounts the angelic message to Joseph, assuring him that the child to be born of Mary would be named Jesus, for He would save His people from their sins. This announcement echoes the prophecies of old, confirming that the long-awaited Savior was about to enter the world. Jesus, whose name signifies salvation, would fulfil the ancient promises and bring redemption to all who believe in Him.

In the later chapters of Matthew, we witness the encounter between Herod and the chief priests and scribes. Herod inquiries about the birthplace of the Messiah, and they respond with the words of the prophet Micah: "In Bethlehem of Judea, for thus it is written by the prophet: 'And you, Bethlehem, in the land of Judah, are by no means least among the rulers of Judah; for from you shall come a ruler who will shepherd my people Israel.'" This interaction further solidifies the connection between the prophecies and the unfolding events surrounding Jesus' birth. Bethlehem, though small in stature, held immense significance as the birthplace of the long-awaited leader and shepherd of Israel.

As we reflect on these prophecies, we are reminded of the meticulous plan of God, woven throughout history, to bring forth His Son, Jesus Christ, into the world. The fulfilment of these ancient words serves as a testament to the faithfulness and sovereignty of God. Through the birth of Jesus, God's promise of salvation was set into motion, offering hope, reconciliation, and eternal life to all who would embrace Him

Study Guide

Remember;

a) There were several prophecies before the birth of Jesus Christ

b) He has been since the world began

c) The purpose of His coming is for the remission of our sins.

d) Focus on the plan of God which Christ came to consummate.

CHAPTER TWO

WHO IS JESUS CHRIST?

The Eternal Word

In the very beginning, before anything else existed, there was God. And present with God was the Word - a distinct yet co-equal Person who was Himself fully God. "In the beginning was the Word, and the Word was with God, and the Word was God" (John 1:1). When God spoke the universe into existence, saying "Let there be light," it was through the Word that creation came into being (Genesis 1:3, John 1:3).

This Word is none other than Jesus Christ Himself, the eternal Son of God. Even from those first verses of Genesis, we see hints of the plurality within the one true God. When God said "Let Us make man in Our image" (Genesis 1:26), it pointed to the Son's role in humanity's creation alongside the Father and Spirit.

Throughout the Old Testament, the coming Messiah or Anointed One was prophesied and prefigured. But when Jesus finally came in the flesh, His identity as the Son of God was proclaimed unmistakably. At His baptism, God's voice from heaven thundered "This is My beloved Son, in whom I am well pleased" (Matthew 3:17). Jesus' baptism revealed the three Persons of the Godhead - the Son being baptized, the Spirit descending like a dove, and the Father's voice speaking from heaven.

The Divine Son

Though He walked the earth as a man, Jesus repeatedly claimed His unique relationship with the Father as the divine Son of God. He asked His disciples the penetrating question - "Who do you say that I am?" While others guessed He might be a prophet, Peter confessed the revealed truth - "You are the Christ, the Son of the living God" (Matthew 16:16). On another occasion, Jesus stated the inescapable implication of His identity - "I and the Father are one" (John 10:30).

The Jewish leaders understood exactly what Jesus was claiming about Himself. At His trial, when the high priest demanded "Are You the Christ, the Son of the Blessed?" Jesus gave the unequivocal response: "I am... and you will see the Son of Man sitting at the right hand of the Power, and coming with the clouds of heaven" (Mark 14:61-62). This was a claim to be the long-awaited Messiah and the Son of God Himself.

In His humanity, Jesus became a "merciful and faithful High Priest" to make atonement for sins (Hebrews 2:17). But He did not glorify Himself for this role. As the writer of Hebrews explains, it was the Father who declared of the Son "You are My Son... You are a priest forever according to the order of Melchizedek" (Hebrews 5:5-6, Psalm 2:7, 110:4). God Himself testified to Jesus' divine Sonship and high priestly ministry.

Jesus has the supreme position as God's Son because He is the perfect revelation of the Father Himself. As Jesus declared, "He who has seen Me has seen the Father" (John 14:9). The Son is the ultimate disclosure of what God is like because the Son shares fully in the nature and being of God. To know Jesus is to know the true and living God.

The Revealed Son

When Jesus asked His disciples "Who do you say that I am?", Simon Peter gave the answer that came not from mere human reasoning, but by revelation from "My Father in heaven" (Matthew 16:16-17). Peter confessed the astounding truth that Jesus is "the Christ, the Son of the living God."

This was the mystery that had been veiled in the Old Testament but now was being unveiled - that the eternal Son of God had taken on human flesh. Even the demons recognized Jesus as "the Son of God" (Luke 4:41), for they could perceive His divine nature and identity.

Jesus is the perfect image and manifestation of the invisible God. As John marvelled, "No one has ever seen God, but the one and only Son, who is himself God and is in closest relationship with the Father, has made him known" (John 1:18). When we look at Jesus Christ, we are seeing the unseen God revealed in human form.

This is why Jesus could make the utterly unique claim, "Anyone who has seen me has seen the Father" (John

14:9). The works Jesus did and the words He spoke were not merely His own, but the Father's - "The Father who dwells in Me does His works" (John 14:10). In Jesus we encounter God Himself, for as Paul wrote, the Son is "the image of the invisible God" (Colossians 1:15).

The Eternal Son Became Man

From eternity past, the Son has been "at the Father's side" (John 1:18), sharing in the glory of God. Yet this eternal Word "became flesh and made his dwelling among us" (John 1:14). The One who was face-to-face with the Father took on human nature and was born as the God-man, Jesus Christ.

This is the supreme expression of God's love - "God so loved the world that he gave his one and only Son, that whoever believes in him shall not perish but have eternal life" (John 3:16). The Father sent His only begotten Son, the beloved One who has eternally been His delight and pleasure, to become a man and die for our sins so that we could have life through Him (1 John 4:9).

As the prophets foretold, this Son would be a King like no other - righteous, victorious, and yet humble, riding on a donkey's colt into Jerusalem (Zechariah 9:9, Matthew 21:1-11). This King is the Lord of glory (1 Corinthians 2:8), the Alpha and Omega, the Beginning and the End (Revelation 22:13). All of God's purposes for creation find their culmination in His Son.

The Son's incarnation was both a profound humbling and a profound exaltation. He existed eternally in the form of God, being Himself fully divine. Yet He willingly "emptied himself, by taking the form of a servant, being born in the likeness of men" (Philippians 2:7). Jesus is the Son who was with the Father before the world existed, and now has returned to the glory He had with the Father, but with our humanity forever joined to His deity (John 17:5).

In the pages of Scripture, we encounter the Son of God who has made the Father known. The Old and New Testaments give a multifaceted witness to the truth that in Christ "the whole fullness of deity dwells bodily" (Colossians 2:9). To know Jesus is to truly know God and to have eternal life.

The Testimony to the Son

From beginning to end, the Scriptures bear witness to Jesus as the eternal Son of God who became incarnate to bring salvation. John made it clear that his gospel account was written "so that you may believe that Jesus is the Messiah, the Son of God, and that by believing you may have life in his name" (John 20:31). To know and believe in Jesus as the divine Son is to have eternal life.

This was the consistent message that the Apostles proclaimed. Peter declared that "all the prophets testify about him that everyone who believes in him receives forgiveness of sins through his name" (Acts 10:43). The prophets looked ahead to the coming Son who would deal with the sin problem once and for all.

The Apostles made bold claims about Jesus' identity and authority as they preached "the word God sent to the people of Israel, telling the good news of peace through Jesus Christ, who is Lord of all" (Acts 10:36). Their message focused on this Jesus as the supreme Lord and divine Son. As Paul summed it up, Jesus is God's "Son...who as to his human nature was a descendant of David, and who through the Spirit of holiness was declared with power to be the Son of God by his resurrection from the dead" (Romans 1:3-4).

The resurrection was the vindicating declaration that Jesus is truly the Son of God. By raising Him from the dead, God put His own stamp of approval on His Son. This is why Peter could cry out boldly to the crowds, "You killed the author of life, but God raised him from the dead. We are witnesses of this" (Acts 3:15). The very ones who crucified the Son of God could not hold Him in death's grip.

Witnesses Ancient and New

Both the ancient Hebrew prophets and the modern-day Apostles agreed on the reality of Jesus as the divine Son. Through His Son, God was accomplishing His plan of redeeming the world and establishing His eternal kingdom rule. This convergence of Old and New Testaments gave a powerful, multifaceted witness to the truth about Jesus Christ.

The prophets foretold a coming King who "having salvation is gentle and riding on a donkey, on a colt, the foal of a donkey" (Zechariah 9:9). The Apostles saw this fulfilled as Jesus entered Jerusalem in humility yet also as the long-awaited Ruler and Son of God (Matthew 21:1-11).

John the Baptist cried out in awe as he saw the Spirit descending on Jesus, "And I have seen and testified that this is the Son of God" (John 1:34). The very voice of God spoke audibly from heaven, "This is my Son, whom I love; with him I am well pleased" (Matthew 3:17). The demons themselves recognized Jesus as "the Holy One of God" and were terrified (Mark 1:24).

Jesus made statements that only the Son of God could rightly make - "I am the Alpha and the Omega...the Beginning and the End" (Revelation 22:13). "I am the bread of life...which comes down from heaven and gives life to the world" (John 6:33,35). The images Jesus used all pointed back to His divine pre-existence and eternal relationship with the Father.

Even under the threat of death, Jesus did not shrink back from declaring His true identity. When the high priest demanded "Are you the Messiah, the Son of the Blessed One?", Jesus responded with the resounding affirmation "I am... And you will see the Son of Man seated at the right hand of Power and coming with the clouds of heaven"

(Mark 14:61-62). He was clearly claiming to be the long-awaited divine Son of God prophesied in Scripture.

Not Blind Chance but Eternal Plan

The New Testament writers understood that Jesus' death was no mere chance occurrence. As Paul wrote, "None of the rulers of this age understood it, for if they had, they would not have crucified the Lord of glory" (1 Corinthians 2:8). Those who condemned Jesus did not grasp that they were killing God's own Son, the glorious Lord of all.

But this was not a tragic mistake - it was the predetermined plan of God. Through the willing sacrifice of His Son on the cross, God was accomplishing the greatest act of love by which sinful humanity could be forgiven and redeemed. As Peter wrote, believers should pay attention "to the words spoken in the past by the holy prophets, and to the command given by our Lord and Savior through your Apostles" (2 Peter 3:2). The coming of the Son was promised long ago and witnessed to by all of Scripture.

In both His words and His works, Jesus demonstrated that He is the Son sent from the Father. He said it clearly - "The works I do in my Father's name testify about me" (John 10:25). His miraculous signs and authority over creation, sickness, demons, and even death revealed His divine identity and sonship. Just as the voice at His baptism declared, this was God's "beloved Son" (Matthew 3:17).

The culminating confirmation came through the resurrection when, as Paul said, Jesus "was declared to be the Son of God in power according to the Spirit of holiness by his resurrection from the dead" (Romans 1:4). What prophet, teacher or supposed son of God has ever conquered death itself? Only Jesus Christ, the true and eternal Son, could emerge victorious from the grave.

All Things Subject to the Son

The Scriptures give a unified witness that this Jesus, God's only Son, has been given the supremacy over all things. As the book of Hebrews celebrates, God has "appointed the Son the heir of all things" (Hebrews 1:2). Paul rejoiced that Jesus "is the image of the invisible God, the firstborn over all creation" and the One "in whom all things hold together" (Colossians 1:15,17).

From the very beginning, through the present age, and into the future culmination, everything has its origin, consistency and purpose in the Son of God. The Apostles preached Jesus as the enthroned Lord who will come again to judge the living and the dead (Acts 10:42). This is the Son who "has on his robe and on his thigh the name written: KING OF KINGS AND LORD OF LORDS" (Revelation 19:16). One day, every knee will bow before the Son who shares in all the glory, honour and power of His Father.

All of Scripture points us to this climactic truth - Jesus is the Son of God, the eternal Word made flesh. To believe in Him is to have life and forgiveness of sins. With the Apostles, the prophets, and heaven's witness, we declare Jesus Christ to be God's only Son who came to reveal the Father's love and bring salvation to the world.

The Highest of All Priests

The Bible reveals that Jesus Christ is far more than just a great teacher, prophet or moral example. He is the eternal Son of God who became the perfect High Priest to make atonement for sins once and for all. As the writer of Hebrews exclaims, "We have a great high priest who has passed through the heavens, Jesus the Son of God!" (Hebrews 4:14)

In the Old Testament priestly system, the high priest would annually enter the Most Holy Place to make atonement for the sins of the people through the sacrifice of animals. But this could never finally deal with sin. It was merely a shadow pointing ahead to the true and greater reality that was to come in Christ.

Jesus is the supreme High Priest, but not from the line of Aaron. Rather, He is "a priest forever, in the order of Melchizedek" (Hebrews 7:17), relating Him to the mysterious priestly figure who blessed Abraham long before the Levitical system was established. As the Son of God, Jesus is the eternal Priest-King, superior to all human priests.

Unlike the Old Testament priests who had to offer sacrifices year after year, Jesus offered a sacrifice once for all time - the sacrifice of Himself (Hebrews 7:27). He did not go through the veil into an earthly Holy of Holies with the blood of animals, but into the very presence of God in heaven with His own blood, to make perfect atonement (Hebrews 9:11-14).

The ultimate sacrifice had to be the unlimited life of the eternal Son of God. Only by giving His own divine life could the debt of sin be paid and true forgiveness achieved. That's why John could declare so assuredly, "He is the atoning sacrifice for our sins, and not only for ours but also for the sins of the whole world" (1 John 2:2).

The Perfect Mediator

Because Jesus is fully God and also took on full humanity, He alone could reconcile God and man. As the God-man, He represents both parties and is the perfect mediator to bring them together. "There is one God and one mediator between God and men, the man Christ Jesus" (1 Timothy 2:5).

Jesus didn't just teach about God or reveal spiritual truths as prophets had done. He blazed the trail to restored relationship with God by giving His life as a ransom to forgive sins (Mark 10:45). Now risen and ascended, Jesus ever lives as our great High Priest, interceding for believers (Hebrews 7:25).

16

No wonder Jesus could make the exclusive claim, "I am the way and the truth and the life. No one comes to the father except through me" (John 14:6). He is the only provision for sinful humans to be forgiven, made right with God, and enter into eternal life. Apart from Jesus, there is no other way.

Someday, this same Jesus who was crucified for sins will return in glory as the King of kings to judge the world (Revelation 19:16). Those who rejected and reviled Him will see Him exalted as the Son of God enthroned at the Father's right hand (Mark 14:62).

Our Confident Access

Because of who Jesus is and what He has done, those who put their faith in Him can now come with bold confidence into God's presence. The veil separating sinful people from a holy God has been torn, and the way into the Most Holy Place has been opened through Christ's blood (Hebrews 10:19-22).

We don't come hesitantly or on the basis of our own righteousness. We come with assurance, because Jesus our great High Priest has gone before us. As the book of Hebrews encourages us, "Therefore, since we have a great high priest who has ascended into heaven, Jesus the Son of God, let us hold firmly to the faith we profess" (Hebrews 4:14).

In Christ, we are welcomed into the very family of God as dearly loved children (1 John 3:1). We can draw near without fear because our sins have been atoned for by the blood of God's own eternal Son. Our confidence is not in ourselves but in the perfect, finished work of our great High Priest, Jesus Christ.

What amazing love the Father has lavished on us! That He would give His only begotten Son to bear our sins and be the atoning sacrifice so that we could be reconciled to God and brought into His eternal fellowship. Jesus alone is the way to the Father because only He is the perfect God-man who resolves our separation from God. Let us hold firmly to this great truth and draw near with confidence through our great High Priest!

From above scriptures in retrospect, we find the following:

Jesus Christ is our King

Jesus Christ is Righteous

Jesus Christ is Victorious (our Salvation)

Jesus Christ is the Son of God

Jesus Christ is the Word of God

Jesus Christ is Lord of all

Jesus is the Judge of all

Jesus Christ is our Lord

Jesus is the Messiah (Anointed Christ)

Jesus is the Author, Source of life

Jesus is our coming King

Jesus is "I AM"

Jesus is our Redeemer

Jesus is our Savior

Jesus Christ is God

Jesus is the Prince of life

Jesus is head over everything for the Church

Jesus rules forever

Jesus gives life and breath to everything

Jesus is our Peace

Jesus is called Wonderful, Counsellor, the Mighty God, the Everlasting Father, and the Prince of Peace

Jesus is the Way, the truth and the Life

Jesus is the Living Bread

Jesus is the Bread of Life

Jesus is the Light of the World

Jesus is our High Priest

Jesus is the one who existed from the beginning

Jesus is the Word of Life

Jesus is our Advocate who pleads our case before the Father

Jesus Christ is the Sacrifice that atones for our sins

Jesus told Thomas, I am the way, the truth, and the life

Jesus is Emmanuel

Jesus is the lord of Glory

Jesus is God's beloved Son

Jesus is the only Begotten Son

Jesus is the Word of God

Jesus is the Alpha and Omega, Beginning and the End, the First and the Last

Jesus is our Passover

Jesus is the Holy one of God

Jesus is the KING of kings and LORD of lords

Jesus is the LORD and SAVIOR

Jesus is the Mediator of the New Covenant

Study Guide

Remember:

a) The Word of God is Eternal

b) Jesus Christ is the Word of God

c) Jesus is the Messiah, Son of the Living God.

d) The eternal Son became man and made His dwelling among us

e) All things are subject to the Son and He is our Redeemer

CHAPTER THREE

RAISED FROM THE DEAD

The Apostles did not follow a mere philosopher or inspirational teacher. They were eyewitnesses to the most pivotal event in all of human history - the resurrection of Jesus Christ from the dead. As Peter boldly declared to the crowds, "We are witnesses of everything he did...They killed him by hanging him on a cross, but God raised him from the dead on the third day...We were those who ate and drank with him after he rose from the dead" (Acts 10:39-41).

This was no fable or fantasy. The Apostles weren't spinning a catchy tale - they were testifying to what their eyes had beheld and their hands had touched (1 John 1:1). These simple men from Galilee lacked the creativity or motive to fabricate such an elaborate mythology. They had nothing to gain from their witness except persecution and martyrdom.

Yet they proclaimed with unwavering conviction that Jesus, the one condemned as a criminal and crucified on a Roman cross, was in fact the eternal Son of God who conquered death by His bodily resurrection. As Peter summarized, Jesus is "the one all the prophets testified about, saying that everyone who believes in him will have their sins forgiven through his name" (Acts 10:43).

Everything Hangs on the Resurrection

The Apostle Paul clearly saw that the truth of Christianity hinges entirely on the reality of the bodily resurrection of Jesus. He wrote to the Corinthians, "And if Christ has not been raised, your faith is futile; you are still in your sins...If only for this life we have hope in Christ, we are of all people most to be pitied" (1 Corinthians 15:17,19).

But Paul joyfully affirmed that Christ has indeed been raised! He was "buried, and... raised on the third day according to the Scriptures" (1 Corinthians 15:4). The prophets and Scriptures had foretold this pivotal event, and the Apostles were now firsthand witnesses that it had come to pass in history. Christ's bodily resurrection was the validation that His atoning death for sin had been accepted by the Father.

Paul marvelled at the implications of the resurrection for all who put their faith in Christ. Though "we were dead in our trespasses," God "made us alive together with Christ" and "raised us up with him and seated us with him in the heavenly places in Christ Jesus" (Ephesians 2:5-6). The overwhelming power that raised Jesus from the grave is now unleashed in the lives of believers (Ephesians 1:19-20).

We have been born again to a living hope through Christ's resurrection (1 Peter 1:3)! Just as the first Adam brought sin and death, the "last Adam" Jesus Christ has brought resurrection life and forgiveness to all who are united with Him by faith (1 Corinthians 15:21-22, 45). As Paul stated,

"God saved you by his grace when you believed" in this glorious gospel of resurrection life through Jesus Christ (Ephesians 2:8).

The Begotten Son of God

Not only did the Apostles witness Jesus' resurrection, but they also saw how it was achieved. To become the Author of eternal salvation, the eternal Son of God had to first humble Himself by taking on human existence (Hebrews 2:10, 5:9). As Paul described, "Though he was in the form of God, [He] did not count equality with God a thing to be grasped, but emptied himself, by taking the form of a servant, being born in the likeness of men" (Philippians 2:6-7).

The eternal Creator became a creature, the unlimited God willingly confined Himself within a human body and human experience. This was an unfathomable condescension of the Son of God for the sake of redeeming fallen humanity. Yet the Son "humbled himself by becoming obedient to the point of death, even death on a cross" (Philippians 2:8). The full extent of His humiliation was suffering the criminal's penalty of execution on a Roman cross.

But that was not the end! Because the Father was pleased with the Son's obedience, He "highly exalted him and bestowed on him the name that is above every name" (Philippians 2:9). The resurrected and glorified Son of God has been enthroned as the ruler over all creation, with every knee bowing before Him in worship. Jesus has reassumed His eternal glory after that temporary, redemptive self-humbling.

The Apostles saw this entire pattern displayed in the incarnate Son of God - His pre-existent glory, His selfless humbling to become a man and die for sins, and finally His exaltation through resurrection and enthronement. They were "witnesses chosen by God in advance" for this world-transforming revelation.

The Apostolic Witness Today

Christ gave the Apostles a solemn charge, as recorded in Acts 10:42 - "He commanded us to preach to the people and to testify that he is the one appointed by God to be judge of the living and the dead." This calling to bear witness to Jesus as the resurrection-conquering Son of God continues today for all who follow Christ.

The church exists as a community of sent ones, commissioned to proclaim to the world this good news that Paul summarized - "Christ died for our sins according to the Scriptures, that he was buried, that he was raised on the third day according to the

Scriptures" (1 Cor 15:3-4). We who have encountered the risen Christ are now His witnesses to this earth-shattering reality.

Like those first eyewitnesses, we testify that because Jesus was raised from the dead, He can raise all who believe in

Him to new, eternal life. This message is the only hope for humanity - that the Son of God in love became a man, died for our sins, conquered death through His resurrection, and now offers forgiveness and new life to all who put their faith in Him as Savior and Lord.

As Paul urged His spiritual son Timothy - "Always remember that Jesus Christ, a descendant of David, was raised from the dead. This is the gospel I preach" (2 Timothy 2:8). Let us never lose sight of the resurrection - the pivot of history that changes everything for those who believe in the Son of God, Jesus Christ. As witnesses to the resurrection, let us bear His light and life to the world!

The Incarnate Son of God

From beginning to end, the Bible testifies that Jesus Christ is no mere man, but the eternal Son of God who became incarnate - taking on human flesh while remaining fully divine. This is the supreme revelation of who God is and the enormity of His love for humanity.

Peter reminded believers that their faith and hope rests entirely on "God, who raised [Christ] from the dead and gave him glory" (1 Peter 1:21). The resurrection powerfully vindicated Jesus' claim to be the Son of God. As John testified, "The Word became flesh and dwelt among us, and we have seen his glory, glory as of the only Son from the Father" (John 1:14). This eternal, glorious Word didn't just visit temporarily, but took on a permanent human nature.

When Philip asked Jesus, "Show us the Father," Jesus gave the astonishing reply: "Whoever has seen me has seen the Father" (John 14:9). He didn't merely teach about God, but embodied God in human form. Jesus could therefore state with absolute authority, "I and the Father are one" (John 10:30). The Jews rightly understood this as a statement of full deity and tried to stone Him for blasphemy (John 10:33).

The Eternal One United with Humanity

This wasn't just a new teaching, but the unveiling of a profound spiritual reality - the eternal Son, who has eternally existed in union and equality with the Father, now united His divine nature with a human nature. As the apostle Paul explained, Christ "though he was in the form of God, did not count equality with God a thing to be grasped, but emptied himself, by taking the form of a servant, being born in the likeness of men" (Philippians 2:6-7).

Jesus was no mere messenger, but the perfect image of the invisible God in bodily form (Colossians 1:15). To see and know Christ was to see and know the Father. This is why Jesus could proclaim, "I am the way, and the truth, and the life. No one comes to the Father except through me" (John 14:6). He was and is the one and only path to restored relationship with God because He alone is both fully God and fully man.

This is the glorious truth foreshadowed in the Old Testament - that the coming Messiah would be none other than God Himself taking on human nature. Throughout the Hebrew scriptures, there are manifestations of this eternal Son, the Word of God who would one day be made flesh. It was the Son who walked with Adam and Eve. It was the Son who appeared to Abraham as Melchizedek, the transcendent king and priest. It was the Son in human form whom Jacob wrestled with at the Jabbok river.

The Son Always Existed to Become Incarnate

From eternity past, the Son was always purposed to become incarnate, to unite His divine nature inseparably with a human one. This was not an afterthought or a Plan B after sin entered the world. No, sin's tragic consequences merely revealed the extent of the Son's unfathomable love and humility in taking the form of a servant.

The incarnate Son perfectly revealed God's heart and character through His life and sacrificial death. The Old Testament priesthood, temple rituals, and sacrificial system all looked forward to and found their fulfilment in the Son becoming the final high priest, the true temple, and the unblemished sacrifice for sins. All of God's promises throughout history culminated in the coming of the incarnate Son of God, Jesus Christ.

No other religious system or worldview has anything close to this remarkable truth about God's Son willingly becoming a man to redeem humanity. Islam views Jesus as merely a prophet, unable to grasp His full divine nature. Eastern religions are based in an impersonal divine force, not a transcendent personal God taking on human existence. Only biblical Christianity exalts the mindboggling truth that the eternal Son has become the God-man.

The incarnation is the basis for the good news that sinful humanity can be forgiven and restored to fellowship with God. Because in Jesus Christ, the chasm between the infinite Creator and finite creatures has been bridged. God yet remains transcendent, while also taking on the frailties and limitations of human existence. The Son of God became like us so that we could become like Him - reconciled children of God.

What heights and depths of love are revealed in the incarnate Son! As the creed proclaims, "God of God, Light of Light, very God of very God...for us and for our salvation he came down from heaven, and was incarnate by the Holy Spirit of the virgin Mary, and was made man." Let us stand in awe of this stupendous truth about the eternal Son uniting His divine nature with ours for our redemption.

Study Guide

Remember:

a) Jesus died for our sins according to the Scriptures, He was buried and He rose again on the third day according to the Scriptures. This is written in 1 Corinthians 15 from 3 through 5.

b) Know who Jesus is for yourself:

- Jesus Christ is the Saviour
- Messiah, Ruler of the Universe
- He is King
- All Authority is given to Him
- The Everlasting God

CHAPTER FOUR

RIGHT STANDING WITH GOD

From the very beginning, humanity was designed to live in perfect relationship and union with God. But the tragic entry of sin shattered that union, separating us from the Source of life itself. We became enslaved to sin's corrupting power, destined for eternal separation from God's peace and joy.

Yet even in that darkest moment, God set in motion His glorious plan to rescue and restore fallen humanity. This restoration would come not through our own effort or merit, but by God's infinite grace flowing to us through faith in His Son Jesus Christ.

The apostle Paul marvelled at this reality - that we can now "be made right with God" apart from keeping the law's demands, which were always insufficient to deal with sin's root problem (Romans 3:21-22). God has done what was impossible for us - He has provided pardon, reconciliation, and new life through the perfect life, atoning death, and resurrection of His Son.

When we place our faith in Jesus Christ, believing that He died for our sins and rose again, we enter into a glorious exchange. Jesus took our sin and shame upon Himself on the cross, while His righteousness is credited to us (2 Corinthians 5:21). We receive the free gift of salvation, not earned by our works or religious pedigree, but solely by God's grace through faith in His Son (Ephesians 2:8-9).

New Life in Christ

At the moment we trust in Christ, something miraculous happens - we are spiritually reborn and brought into vital union with Jesus Himself. As Paul wrote, "If anyone is in Christ, he is a new creation. The old has passed away; behold, the new has come" (2 Corinthians 5:17). Our old life dominated by sin and separation from God is exchanged for new resurrection life in Christ.

We are not simply turned over a fresh moral leaf, but we receive the very life and Spirit of Christ implanted within us. Paul exclaimed to believers, "You are the body of Christ and individually members of it" (1 Corinthians 12:27). What an astonishing privilege - to be incorporated into the body of Christ Himself, with His own Spirit animating and empowering us for abundant life!

Because of this spiritual union, everything changes. "The law of the Spirit of life has set you free in Christ Jesus from the law of sin and death" (Romans 8:2). The tyranny of sin's reign has been broken through our co-crucifixion and resurrection with Christ. His victory has become our victory as we surrender to His lordship.

Living in Union with Christ

To be "in Christ" is to have our entire identity transformed. We are no longer defined by our sins, failures, ethnicity or any other human distinctions. Our primary identity is now that we belong to Christ, having been purchased by His blood (1 Corinthians 6:20). We are His possession, His beloved bride, united with Him in an unfathomable spiritual union.

This does not mean we lose our individuality or personal agency. Rather, it means we now live in the glorious freedom of having Christ's own life and power pulsing within us. As Paul wrote, we are to "work out your own salvation with fear and trembling, for it is God who works in you, both to will and to work for his good pleasure" (Philippians 2:12-13). The very desires and energy come from Christ's indwelling presence.

Those in Christ are called to "walk in a manner worthy of the Lord, fully pleasing to him: bearing fruit in every good work and increasing in the knowledge of God" (Colossians 1:10). Every virtue, every act of service and love, every spiritual growth that occurs in believers is really an expression of Christ's own life within us. As Paul exulted, "I can do all things through him who strengthens me" (Philippians 4:13).

So we boast not in ourselves, but solely in Jesus Christ. We "acknowledge every grace which is ours in Christ Jesus" (1 Corinthians 1:4). He alone is our righteousness, wisdom, sanctification and redemption (1 Corinthians 1:30). All glory belongs to Him who has rescued us from sin's dominion and made us new creations in Himself. That is the unfathomable privilege of those who have been united with Christ through faith!

Partakers of Christ's Divine Nature

When we put our faith in Jesus Christ, something radical happens - we are spiritually reborn and brought into vital union with Him. The apostle Paul declared with awe, "If anyone is in Christ, he is a new creation. The old has passed away; behold, the new has come!" (2 Corinthians 5:17).

This isn't merely turning over a fresh moral leaf, but receiving the very life and divine nature of Christ Himself implanted within our spirits. We become "partakers of the divine nature" (2 Peter 1:4), joined inseparably to Christ as members of His own body (Ephesians 5:30).

Paul rejoiced that believers are heirs of God and "joint heirs with Christ" to share in all He has inherited from the Father (Romans 8:17). We don't just receive some spiritual benefits - we are brought into the same living relationship with the Father that Christ enjoys as the eternal Son! As John marvelled, "See what kind of love the Father has given to us, that we should be called children of God; and so we are" (1 John 3:1).

Study Guide

Remember;

a) Born again believers have a right standing with God through our union with Jesus.
b) We are the righteousness of God in Christ
c) As He is so are we now

CHAPTER FIVE

CRUCIFIED AND RESURRECTED WITH CHRIST

This unfathomable union only becomes possible because of what Christ accomplished through His death, burial and resurrection. When He died on the cross, we died with Him - our "old self was crucified with him" so that we would no longer be enslaved to sin (Romans 6:6).

We then were spiritually "buried with him through baptism into death" (Romans 6:4), laying our old sinful nature in the grave, just as Christ's body was buried after His death. This is why baptism by immersion so powerfully symbolizes our identification with Christ's own death, burial and resurrection.

But we don't remain entombed in death! Just as the Father raised Christ in resurrection power and glory, so we too have been "raised up with him" and now share in His resurrection life (Ephesians 2:6). The same mighty power that brought Christ out of the grave now courses within us through the indwelling Holy Spirit (Ephesians 1:19-20).

No wonder Paul could declare that just as Christ lives, we too "will also live with him" (Romans 6:8) by virtue of our spiritual union with Him. Our old sinful self has been crucified and buried. Our new redeemed self has been resurrected in Christ!

One with the Righteous One

Because we are now "in Christ," clothed in His very righteousness, we stand perfect and blameless before God. There is no more condemnation and the devil has "no evidence" to accuse us (Romans 8:1, Revelation 12:10). Despite our former guilty state, we have been completely justified - put in right standing with God - not by works, but by faith in the finished work of Christ on our behalf (Romans 3:28, 5:1).

Paul exulted that Christ "became to us righteousness and sanctification and redemption" (1 Corinthians 1:30). As those united with the Righteous One Himself, we are reckoned as righteous in God's sight. This doesn't make us robotically perfect, but it does change our fundamental identity and open up brand new possibilities for righteous living.

No longer defined by our past sins, weaknesses or ethnic backgrounds, our primary identity is now "in Christ" as forgiven children of God (Galatians 3:26-28). He is our life source, our wisdom, our sanctification, our reconciliation with the Father (1 Corinthians 1:30, Colossians 3:4). We are privileged to share in the same intimate relationship that Christ has always enjoyed with His Father. We can experience the abundant spiritual riches that are ours in Him (Ephesians 1:3).

All Treasures Inherited in Christ

Because Christ is Lord over all creation (Colossians 1:15-18), those united with Him inherit all spiritual blessings in

Him (Ephesians 1:3). We have been raised up with Christ and "seated with him in the heavenly places" (Ephesians 2:6), given authority in spiritual realms, reigning over principalities and powers that once enslaved us (Ephesians 1:21).

We need no longer live powerless, defeated lives, trapped in sin's dominion. Christ's resurrection power is now ours (Philippians 3:10). We are "more than conquerors" through spiritual union with the victorious Christ (Romans 8:37). His divine life and energy is working within us, enabling us to do "far more abundantly than all we ask or think" (Ephesians 3:20).

 What a glorious reality - to be "in Christ" as a new creation, partaking of His very nature and all the treasures that He possesses! Our old identities have passed away. We are royalty now, God's beloved children, ambassadors of the King of kings. His Spirit bears witness with our spirits that we are heirs of God, destined for glorification just as Christ has been glorified (Romans 8:16-17).

Let this truth firmly plant itself in our minds and hearts. When we experience weakness, we can remember "I can do all things through Christ who strengthens me" (Philippians 4:13). When accusations come, we overcome them by the blood of the Lamb and the word of our testimony that we are the righteousness of God in Christ (Revelation 12:11). We reign in life through spiritual union with Christ our Overcomer, Redeemer and Righteousness (Romans 5:17).

Confessing Christ as Lord

At the core of the gospel message is the call to confess Jesus Christ as Lord and Savior. This isn't merely an intellectual assent to facts about Jesus, but a whole-life surrender to His rightful rulership. As the apostle Paul wrote, "If you confess with your mouth that Jesus is Lord and believe in your heart that God raised him from the dead, you will be saved" (Romans 10:9).

To receive salvation, we must acknowledge Jesus as the divine Son of God, who died for our sins and conquered death through His resurrection. But we must go further than mental belief - we must enthrone Jesus as the Lord who is now in charge of our daily lives. This is the very heart of the gospel - transferring the rule and mastery over our lives from our own sinful selves to the Lordship of Christ.

When we confess Jesus as Lord from a sincere heart, everything changes. The old sinful self-dies with Christ and we are raised to walk in "newness of life" (Romans 6:4). We become "new creatures in Christ" with our past sins blotted out, never to be remembered against us (2 Corinthians 5:17, Isaiah 43:25). Our history of missing God's mark is wiped clean through Christ's blood.

This spiritual rebirth and fresh start occur not through any works of our own, but solely through faith in what Christ has already accomplished. The law could never make anyone righteous before God, but could only expose our sinfulness (Romans 3:20). We cannot earn or merit our righteousness through religious duties and rule-keeping.

But the amazing news is that God has made "a way of righteousness apart from the law" (Romans 3:21). Through our faith in Jesus Christ, His very own perfect righteousness is credited to us (Romans 3:22). This right standing before God is not anything we achieve, but is a free gift received by grace through faith in Christ's finished work on our behalf (Romans 3:24).

Our own feeble attempts at self-righteousness are as filthy rags before a holy God (Isaiah 64:6). How liberating that we don't have to strive and toil to measure up! We simply receive by faith the free gift of right standing before God that comes through Christ's atoning death and victorious resurrection (Romans 4:24-25).

Study Guide

Remember;

    a)   By faith, Christ now lives in the believer

    b)   Our duty is to stand on God's Word and live in it

CHAPTER SIX

OUR IDENTITY

When we confess Jesus as Lord and put our faith in Him, we take on a whole new identity. We shed our old selves defined by ethnicity, family history and past failures. Our primary identity is now as cherished children of God, born again into His royal family as "a chosen race, a royal priesthood, a holy nation, a people for God's own possession" (1 Peter 2:9).

The old limiting labels no longer apply! We are not "nobodies" but "somebody" in Christ (1 Peter 2:10). God's regenerating power courses through our spiritual veins, altering our spiritual DNA so that we now share the very nature and qualities of Christ Himself. No more need for inferiority, shame or weakness - we are recreated to be overcomers who walk in the glorious freedom of who we are in Christ.

The gospel announces that through union with Christ, we are no longer enslaved to sin's dominion but liberated to "walk in newness of life" and "bear fruit for God" (Romans 7:4, 6). Jesus becomes our wisdom, righteousness, sanctification and redemption (1 Corinthians 1:30). His death destroyed the power of death, and His resurrection life now pulsates within us (2 Timothy 1:10).

We are not just forgiven, but made entirely new creations who can reign in life through the power of Christ's indwelling presence (Romans 5:17). What a glorious reality! Let us never shrink back from embracing our new identities as overcomers, royalty, and possessors of every spiritual blessing in Christ. By His grace, we are who He has made us to be

You have powerfully captured the glorious truth that we are justified - made righteous before God - not by any works of our own, but solely through faith in Jesus Christ and what He accomplished on the cross. This is the very heart of the gospel message. Here is an expanded look at this freeing doctrine.

Study Guide

Remember;

a) Who you are in Christ now

b) You have a new identity, new nature in Christ. Past sins, guilt are taken out of the way. Your sins are forever remitted

c) Your heart is now the heart of flesh and the Holy Spirit lives in you forever

d) Now, see yourselves in the image of God.

e) You can now live right without being tied to sinful lifestyle

CHAPTER SEVEN

THE COURTROOM GRACE

The Bible paints the picture of humanity standing before God's courtroom, guilty of violating His holy laws and deserving just condemnation. We have all sinned and fallen short of God's perfect standard (Romans 3:23). On our own merits, there is no defences we could possibly make. We are spiritually bankrupt before the Judge of all the earth.

Yet at the very moment we deserve the gavel's verdict against us, God does something astounding. He steps down from the judge's bench and in "the mystery of the gospel" (Ephesians 6:19), takes our place in the defendant's chair. The righteous Judge becomes the guilty one and willingly suffers sin's penalty on our behalf through the sacrifice of His Son on the cross.

But that is only half of the picture. Just as significantly, God "justifies the one who has faith in Jesus" (Romans 3:26). Through our faith in Christ's finished work for us, God the righteous Judge issues an unmerited verdict of "not guilty" and freely "justifies the ungodly" (Romans 4:5). He clothes us in the righteousness of Christ Himself, so that now in His eyes we appear just as perfect and flawless as His Son.

The Judge was judged in our place, so that we could receive His righteousness and justification as a free gift by grace through faith (Romans 3:24). What a scandalous exchange! As Charles Spurgeon exclaimed, "He was condemned for our sins, in which He had no share, that we might be justified by His righteousness, in which we had no share."

Justified by His Blood

This great transfer could only happen because of Christ's infinitely-valuable blood, shed for us on the cross. His death fully "satisfied" God's wrath against sin, appeasing or "propitiating" the just requirements of God's holiness (Romans 3:25). By faith in that sacrificial blood, our sins can be completely forgiven and God's righteous character is upheld and vindicated.

Peter rejoiced that we have been "ransomed" by the "precious blood of Christ, like that of a lamb without blemish or spot" (1 Peter 1:18-19). Guilty sinners have been purchased out of the slave market of sin, redeemed by God's own Son becoming our spotless sacrificial substitute. The redemption price has been infinitely paid!

Only the sinless Son of God could become this perfect atoning sacrifice to satisfy God's justice and reconcile us to the Father. When we put our trust in this redeeming work of Christ, the guilt, penalty and power of sin is broken over our lives. We are forever justified in God's sight through the "abundance of grace and the free gift of righteousness" (Romans 5:17).

No Condemnation for the Justified

To be justified means we can now enter God's presence confidently, free from all sense of guilt, shame or condemnation. As Paul exulted, "There is therefore now no condemnation for those who are in Christ Jesus" (Romans 8:1). The record of debt has been entirely cancelled, never to be held against us again (Colossians 2:13-14).

This unshakable position of being "justified by faith" (Romans 5:1) gives the believer a permanent standing of peace and favour with God. We are not made righteous through our feeble attempts at rule keeping or religious observances. It is "not because of works but because of his call" that we have been made eternally right with God (Romans 9:11).

Free from the futile treadmill of trying to justify ourselves, we can now live in the freedom and joy of being fully accepted by God because of Christ's finished work. We are God's beloved children, lavished with the "riches of his grace" and assured of our eternal inheritance (Ephesians 1:5-7).

What motivates us now is not a joyless sense of obligation, but overflowing thankfulness that "while we were still sinners, Christ died for the ungodly" (Romans 5:8). His sacrifice has forever settled our case before God's bar of justice. Let us live rejoicing in this status of being permanently justified by grace through faith in Jesus Christ!

Our friendship with God as believers has been restored through the sacrificial death of His Son, Jesus Christ. While we were once enemies of God, we are now heirs of His kingdom and joint heirs with Jesus. This incredible truth allows us to rejoice in our newfound relationship with God, as we have been made friends of God through the redemptive work of Jesus Christ.

According to Romans 5:11, if you are saved, you are no longer considered an enemy of God but a friend. Righteousness is now a gift that we receive freely, and we are no longer under the dominion of sin but under the grace of God. When Jesus was raised from the dead, we were declared righteous, and through His abundant grace, we have been given right standing with God, resulting in eternal life through Jesus Christ our Lord.

The gift of grace is truly generous and lifegiving, offering forgiveness, righteousness, and eternal life to all who receive it. We are called to embrace this gift and experience God's best for our lives. Just as Adam's trespass brought death to many, the grace of God through Jesus Christ overflows to all, bringing life and freedom from sin.

As believers, we are called to reign as kings in this life, reigning over sin, pain, poverty, and sickness through our righteousness in Christ. This consciousness of righteousness sets us free from the power of sin, allowing us to live in the freedom of God's grace. We have the power to pursue holiness and eternal life, knowing that God no longer counts our sins against us but offers us reconciliation through Christ.

Through Christ, we are made right with God and have the Spirit of God living within us, giving us the power to overcome our natural influences and live victoriously in Christ. We can confidently declare that we are crucified with Christ, yet we live by faith in Him, knowing that He loves us and has given Himself for us.

In Christ, we are redeemed, saved, righteous, blessed, healed, and triumphant. We are no longer defined by our past, emotions, anger, or habits, but by our identity in Christ as children of God. Let us embrace this truth and walk in the fullness of our inheritance as sons and daughters of the Most High God. Glory to God! Amen.

Beloved, before you even accepted Him or will accept Him, know that He loves you unconditionally and eternally. His love for you is constant and unwavering, regardless of your past, present, or future actions. This love is demonstrated through the sacrifice of Jesus Christ, who died for our sins so that we may have eternal life.

In Romans 5:17, we are reminded that through the abundance of grace and the gift of righteousness, we can reign in life by Jesus Christ. This reign is not based on our own efforts or merits, but on the righteousness of God that we receive through faith in Christ. As believers, we are called to reign as righteousness kings in our domain, speaking life and truth into our circumstances.

As blood-bought, blood-washed, born-again children of God, we have been saved from sin and restored to fellowship and favour with God through faith in the blood of Jesus. Salvation is a free gift that is available to all who believe in the Lord Jesus Christ and accept Him as their Savior.

Righteousness, as Brother Kenneth E. Hagin explains, is not something we earn through good deeds or right living. It is a gift that we receive through the new birth, when we believe in Jesus and receive His life and nature within us. This divine nature makes us righteous in the eyes of God, allowing us to stand before Him without condemnation or inferiority.

Through faith in Jesus Christ, we become the righteousness of God and are called to walk in the light as children of God. Jesus, who is righteous, became our righteousness so that we may have a right standing with God and access to His presence without fear or shame.

In 1 Corinthians 1:30, we are reminded that we can stand before God as though we had never sinned, without any sense of condemnation or inferiority. Each believer has the same standing with God and is equally righteous in His sight. By knowing who we are in Christ, what we have in Him, and what we can do through Him, we can confidently walk in our identity as children of God and heirs of His kingdom.

Let us embrace the gift of righteousness, walk in the light of His love, and reign in life through the grace and power of Jesus Christ. May we live out our identity as righteousness kings, shining brightly as lights in a dark world and proclaiming the truth of God's love and salvation to all. Amen.

Study Guide

Remember;

a) Grace is a gift

b) Your justification is through the Blood of Jesus

c) Salvation is a change in NATURE

d) Salvation is free

CHAPTER EIGHT

SALVATION

Every man is a sinner outside of Christ, as stated in Romans 3:23, "For all have sinned and come short of the glory of God." This truth highlights the universal need for a Savior to reconcile us to God and restore us to a right relationship with Him. In His infinite love and mercy, God chose to intimately connect Himself with the Church, which is the body of Christ. Through the sacrifice of Jesus, we are made righteous and able to stand in the presence of God as though we had never sinned.

Ephesians 2:12-13 paints a vivid picture of the state of an unbeliever - someone who is without Christ, without hope, and without God in this world. This individual is described as an alien from the commonwealth of Israel, a stranger to the covenants of promise, and ultimately separated from the true source of hope and salvation. Without a relationship with God, there is a void that cannot be filled by anything in this world.

The absence of hope signifies a lack of connection to Christ and God the Father. Without hope of eternal glory, one remains lost and disconnected from the divine purpose for which they were created. However, the transformative power of Christ changes everything. As Colossians 1:27 declares, "Christ in you is the hope of glory." This profound truth reveals that the presence of

Christ within a believer is the assurance of eternal glory and the promise of a restored relationship with God.

Through faith in Jesus Christ, we are no longer strangers or aliens but are adopted into the family of God. We are given a new identity as children of God, heirs of His kingdom, and recipients of His grace and mercy. The hope of eternal glory shines brightly within us, guiding our steps and illuminating the path to a life of purpose, fulfilment, and joy.

As believers, we are called to share this message of hope and redemption with those who are still lost and without Christ. We are ambassadors of reconciliation, proclaiming the good news of salvation and inviting others to experience the transformative power of God's love.

Let us embrace our identity as children of God, walking in the light of His truth and shining brightly as beacons of hope in a world that desperately needs the saving grace of Jesus Christ. Amen.

In John 16:7-11, Jesus speaks about the importance of His departure and the coming of the Holy Spirit. He tells His disciples that it is necessary for Him to go away so that the Comforter, the Holy Spirit, can come to them. When the Holy Spirit comes, He will convict the world of sin, righteousness, and judgment.

In verse 9, Jesus specifically mentions that the Holy Spirit will convict the world of sin because they do not believe in Him. This highlights the fundamental sin of rejecting Jesus as the Savior and Lord. It is not about confessing every individual sin but about acknowledging the need for Jesus in our lives.

Salvation is not about what we can do or give up, but about believing in Jesus and confessing Him as Lord. The sinner's guilt is ultimately rooted in rejecting Jesus, and salvation comes through confessing His lordship and surrendering to His control in our daily lives.

Titus 2:11 emphasizes that the grace of God, which brings salvation, is available to all mankind. It is through this grace that we are saved, not by our own efforts or works. Our justification, or being declared righteous, comes freely through faith in Jesus Christ and God's unmerited favour.

The heart of the gospel, as Brother Kenneth Hagin points out, lies in confessing the lordship of Jesus Christ. This confession is not just a one-time event but a continual surrender to His will and authority in our lives. It is through this confession that we experience true transformation and salvation.

As sinners, we are unable to save ourselves or meet God's perfect standards. Our only hope lies in placing our faith in Jesus Christ, who paid the price for our sins and offers us the gift of salvation through His grace. Let us embrace this gift with gratitude and live out our faith by confessing Jesus as Lord and allowing His Spirit to guide and empower us on our journey of faith. Amen.

Romans 5:20 reminds us that the Ten Commandments were given to show us the extent of our failure to obey God's law. However, as we recognize our sinfulness, we also see the abundance of God's grace and forgiveness. It is not about cleaning ourselves up before coming to Christ, but about accepting His cleansing and becoming new creations in Him, as 2 Corinthians 5:17 tells us.

Once we are born again, God begins a transformation in our lives, empowering us to make changes and live according to His will. In Matthew 10:32-33, we are reminded of the importance of publicly acknowledging our relationship with Christ and the promise of His acknowledgment before the Father in heaven.

As believers, our prayer life is centred on knowing Christ more deeply. We are encouraged to pray the Pauline prayers found in Ephesians chapters 1-3, seeking a deeper relationship with Him. Responding to God's love involves believing in Him and inviting Him into every aspect of our lives, allowing His redemption to make us children of God, as John 1:12 reveals.

The steps to salvation are outlined for us to follow: acknowledging our sinfulness, repenting and turning to God, confessing Jesus as Lord, forsaking sin, believing in Him as Savior and Lord, inviting Him into our hearts, and experiencing the indwelling of the Holy Spirit. Through these steps, we receive the gift of eternal life and cross over from death to life, as promised in John 5:24.

Study Guide

Remember;

a) You're to make Him Saviour and Lord of your life
b) He can cleanse you and end your years of guilt and shame
c) He can end your struggles with addiction, substance use, alcoholism, pornography, lesbianism, gambling and all vices.
d) You can be live to please Him

CONCLUSION

In conclusion, according to 1 Peter 1:25. "But the word of the Lord remains forever. And that word is the Good News that is been preached to you."

"Hold fast the form of sound word which you have heard of me, in faith and love which is in Christ Jesus" 2 Timothy 1:13.

"And now, dear children remain in fellowship with Christ so that when he returns, you will be full of courage and not shrink back from him in shame" 1 John 2:28, 29.

Since we know that Christ is righteous, we also known that all who do what is right are God's children. Praise God, we are God's children and we will not shrink back from Him at His return. In John 15:5 Jesus says "He is the vine; you are the branches. Those who remain in me and I in them, will produce much fruit. For apart from me you can do nothing. We all need Him to fulfil destiny. Glory to God forever!

a

DECISION FOR CHRIST

Do you know Jesus as your Savior and Lord of your life? The only person to answer this question is you.

"Turn to me and be saved, all the ends of the earth; For I am God, and there is no other." Isaiah 45:22. Salvation is based on the Christian being the recipient of God's saving action. The living message is the revelation of faith for salvation. You must publicly declare with your mouth that Jesus is Lord and believe in your heart that God raise Him from the death, to experience salvation. Then you will never be disappointed because of you believe in Him.

SAY THIS PRAYER

Heavenly father, I come to you in the Name of Jesus. Thank you for loving me. Thank you for sending your son to die for me. I recognize that I am a sinner. Your word says, "whosoever shall call on the name of the Lord shall be saved" (Acts 2:2). I am calling on you, Jesus, come into my heart and be my Savior and Lord according to Romans 10:9-10.

Cleanse me and purge me with your precious Blood and write my name in the Book of life. I thank you LORD for delivering me from the power of Satan and darkness and bringing me to the Kingdom of your dear Son.

Today I accept JESUS as my Savior and confess Him as my LORD. I surrender the control of my life to Him from today. Thank You LORD! I am born again.

The Angels always rejoices when a soul is won into the Kingdom of God (Luke 15:7). I know now there is great rejoicing because you have become His son. This implies you can now walk with God and please Him Just as Jesus is the Son of God and lived on earth to please the Father, He died so we can be sons of God. You are now a son of God if you prayed the above prayer. Shine your light!

ABOUT THE AUTHOR

Mandy Adebayo is the Chief Executive Officer of Movina Values. She holds a doctorate of philosophy in counselling. She is an itinerant minister of the Gospel and an entrepreneur.